Dear reader-person,

Since I am probably the *World's Greatest Criminal*, I have decided to share my stories with you.

I have **A LOT of them** and I'm excited about getting them into the world.

This **first** volume has a story about an *unbelievably* beautiful painting, and then another one about a watermelon-growing competition.

I'm the hero of the stories. **Obviously!**

Welcome to my books!

- Devil Cat
  (Master Criminal)

www.itsdevilcat.com

Contents

MAIN CHARACTERS

DEVIL-CAT

Pizza-lover
Chaos-causer
Master-burglar

General, all round villain

The **GREATEST** criminal
<u>*ever*</u>!

Age: Unknown

Height: 5 ft
Weight: 122 lbs (55 kgs)
Number of tails: 2

Favourite food: Pizza, carrots, sardine-flavored ice-cream

Favourite drink: Smiley-Cola, carrot juice

Terrified of: Watermelons
Main hobby: Sleeping
Hours of sleep per day: 16

BUNNY-FACE

Devil-Cat's *arch-enemy*
CRAFTY
Patient

Age: Unknown
Height: 4ft
Weight: 110 lbs (49 kgs)
Number of tails: 1

Favourite food: *Everything*
Favourite drink: Smiley-cola

Terrified of: Falling cakes
Main hobby: Watching TV
Hours of sleep per day: 12

THE BALD BOG-SLOTNIGG BROTHERS

* Friends of Bunny-Face
* Twins
* **Not** *super-smart*

Age: Unknown
Height: 5ft
Weight: Bruno 165 lbs (75 kgs)
         Boris 174 lbs (79 kgs)

Number of tails: We haven't checked but *zero* we imagine

Favourite food: Maggot pie
Favourite drink: Smiley-cola

Terrified of: Cockroaches
Main hobby: Art
Hours of sleep per day: Unknown

The Disapppearing Duck

Devil-Cat was visiting the national gallery...

...because he wanted to see a famous painting:

The Duckworth Blue!

The world's most famous painting...

...of a duck!

Devil-Cat was stunned.

In fact for the first time in his life he was <u>speechless</u>!

But then some *thoughts* began to form in his head...

...and then some *words*.

③ COPY THE PHOTO TO MAKE A PERFECT REPLICA.

④ ROLL UP THE REPLICA.

⑦ GET INTO THE GALLERY BY PRETENDING TO BE COMING TO FIX SOMETHING.

SURE, COME ON IN!

GUARD

So Devil-Cat got to work.

26

27

Weeks and weeks
of painting
passed.

PAINT
PAINT
PAINT
PAINT
PAINT
PAINT
PAINT
PAINT
PAINT
PAINT
PAINT"

Months passed.

PAINT PAINT PAINT PAINT PAINT PAINT PAINT PAINT PAINT PAINT PAINT PAINT PAINT PAINT PAINT PAINT PAINT

And so Devil-Cat did what he'd planned to do.

A *very* happy Devil-Cat indeed.

Back at the gallery, the curator, Mr. Hemington-Hemington-Hemington, noticed the fraud immediately.

But despite having the best
police on the case...

...there were simply no clues.

Dr. Hemington-Hemington-
Hemington had no choice
but to be patient.

The painting would show up
eventually.

The funny thing was, no-one else seemed to notice the difference.

② USING THE PHOTO, i PAINT A PERFECT COPY.

③ I'LL THEN ROLL IT UP AnD Hide IT IN MY BICYCLE.

④ THEN DRESS UP AS aN ELECTRICIAN...

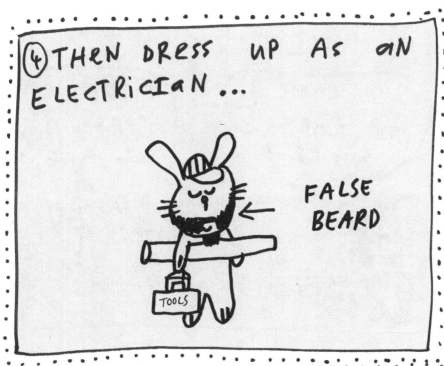

FALSE BEARD

⑤ ...aND RIDE OVER TO DEVIL-CAT'S HOUSE.

And so Bunny-Face got to work.

Show us
Bunny-Face!

56

And with that, he hid it in his bicycle, put on his disguise, and went over to Devil-Cat's house.

And it worked!

Without Devil-Cat noticing, Bunny-Face made the swap!

Mission accomplished!

Back at Bunny-Face's house:

**And Bunny-Face was right,
Devil-Cat noticed nothing.**

A few weeks
passed.

Then one night, the bald Bog-Slotnigg brothers went over to Bunny-Face's place for an evening of take-outs (pizza) and TV.

First Bruno noticed the painting.

Then Boris did.

When Bunny-Face went into the kitchen:
THAT IS THE MOST AMAZING PAINTING I HAVE EVER SEEN!!
ME TOO!!
WE'LL HAVE TO BUY IT FROM BUNNY-FACE.

BUY IT? CRIMINALS LIKE US DON'T BUY THINGS, WE STEAL THEM!
EVEN FROM FRIENDS?
EVEN FROM FRIENDS!!

67

The bald Bog-Slotnigg brothers rushed home and got to work.

Soon their plan was done.

This is what it
looked like.

At this point dear reader, since their handwriting is so terrible, we'll translate it for you.

(1) From memory we paint our own version of the painting.

(2) We then hide our painting
    in a vacuum cleaner.

(3) We then dress up as
    carpet cleaners.

(4) We then go to
    Bunny-Face's house.

(5) He'll let us in.

(6) When he's not looking,
    we swap the paintings.

(7) He'll notice nothing!

And so the bald Bog-Slotnigg brothers got to work.

It took them just fifteen
minutes to finish it.

Show us, bald
Bog-Slotnigg
brothers,
show us!

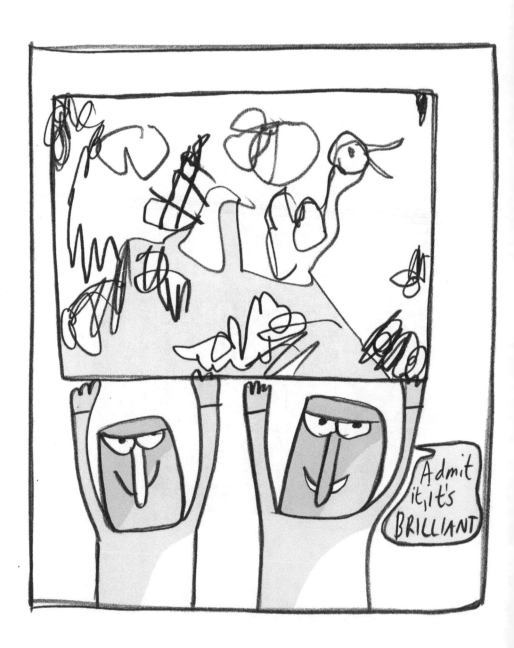

With the painting done, they got into action. They rolled it up and stuffed it into a vacuum cleaner...

...put on their disguises...

Once inside, when Bunny-Face wasn't looking, a quick swap.

Back at home:

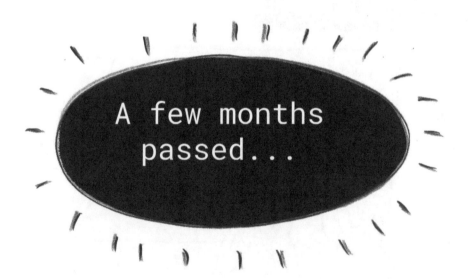

...until one day when the curator of the national gallery, Dr. Hemington-Hemington-Hemington, happened to walk past the bald Bog-Slotnigg brothers' house...

AHA, THE THIEVES!

And so Dr. Hemington-
Hemington-Hemington
hatched a plan.

He shot off to the gallery.

And rolled up Devil-Cat's replica and popped it into a tube.

He then went back to his house...

...where he called for his favorite three cockroaches. And yes, he has pet cockroaches. Over four thousand of them.

With them on board, he shot back to the bald Bogg-Slotnigg brothers' house...

...where he popped Clive, Colin and Crosby in through a window.

He then went and knocked on
the front door.

At which point Clive, Colin and Crosby arrived underfoot!!

Dr. Hemington-Hemington-Hemington sauntered inside...

...swapped the paintings...

...and left. With the true original under his arm.

And
so here's
where the
story ends.

The original masterpiece
was back in the
national gallery.

Bunny-Face's dreadful copy was at Devil-Cat's house.

And Devil-Cat's awful copy was at the bald Bog-Slotnigg brother's house.

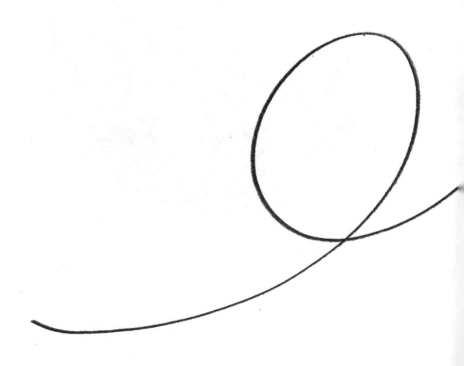

The end

Story 2

The Battle of the Watermelons

*This story is
also known as:*

How Devil-Cat
got to be
COMPLETELY &
UTTERLY & <u>TOTALLY</u>
Terrified
of Watermelons

Lots of excitement in town today, because...

...it was the time of year for the *World Watermelon Growing* Chamionships!

You obviously have
heard of this
EPIC event?

But just to refresh
your memory, here are
some details.

And a watering-can.

And a watermelon *seed.*

They then have EXACTLY *a month* to grow their watermelon.

On the *final day*, they pick their melon...

...and present it for inspection at the competition tent.

The President flies in and presents the prizes.

There are a bunch of
different categories:

One for the WEIRDEST
watermelon.

Then one for the THINNEST.

Then one for the SQUAREST.

But the GRAND-PRIZE is reserved for the LARGEST!

And this prize is *not just a trophy*, but also a LIFETIME supply of *FREE* watermelon juice!

So obviously he entered.

And obviously he wanted to win.

Wouldn't you want a free lifetime supply of watermelon juice?

By the end of week one, his melon was doing alright, but not brilliantly.

There were some bigger melons around for sure.

Even Bunny-Face, his arch-enemy, had a bigger one.

122

And so he got to work.

Turns out that it wasn't *that* easy-peasy lemon-squeezy.

The first potion made things <u>go spotty</u>.

The second made things <u>vibrate</u>.

The third <u>transformed things into bananas</u>.

The fourth made things <u>float</u>.

The fifth made them <u>shrink</u>.

He had to make sure to use a *small amount* otherwise people would get suspicious.

Devil-Cat poured a few drops of *Fast-Grow* potion into his potion-proof watering can.

...and began to water his melon.

The effect was *immediate.*

People crowded around.

Bunny-Face, who *of course* also wanted to win, was not impressed.

Not impressed at all.

So Bunny-Face disguised
himself as a bush...

...and shuffled over to
Devil-Cat's plot.

He was there all day, watching Devil-Cat's *every* move.

But since the *Fast-Grow* potion was already in the watering can, he couldn't spot anything amiss.

Bunny-Face got to work.

142

③ IT WILL BE FULL OF CLEVER COGS + MACHINERY...

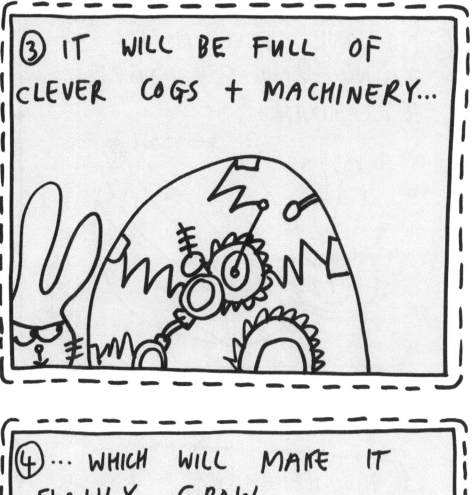

④ ... WHICH WILL MAKE IT SLOWLY GROW.

And this is *exactly*
what he did.

Bunny-Face got to work.

Finally, after a week:

Meanwhile, Devil-Cat's watermelon was huge.

That night Bunny-Face swapped his *old*, normal watermelon for his **new** mechanical one.

He tapped a few buttons on the remote...

...and with a *whirr* and a *click*, it began to grow.

Slowly, *slowly*, it grew and grew.

By the end of week three, it was almost as large as Devil-Cat's.

Over the next few days, the gap narrowed.

DEVIL-CAT'S IS SLIGHTLY BIGGER
↓

With just **three** days to go, Bunny-Face's watermelon took the lead.

The crowd was excited, but Devil-Cat was not.

By the next day, he was in the lead again.

Bunny-Face, annoyed, set his watermelon to grow faster.

Within hours, he was ahead.

Devil-Cat added even more potion.

Now he was ahead.

This *tit-for-tat* ensued all day.

WHIRR
CLICK

But then Bunny-Face's
lead started growing.

Devil-Cat panicked and put
in <u>too much</u> potion.

Devil-Cat was sent flying!

164

The explosion was SO big that the competition tent *was completely ruined.*

And *every* watermelon was damaged.

During the chaos,
Bunny-Face escaped.

But his melon did not. It was confiscated by the police.

The President arrived.

But then *something unexpected* happened.

175

And *why*, you might ask, did he turn down the prize?

..and not because he wants others to enjoy the free gift...

...but because, from that day on, due to the explosion, Devil-Cat was **COMPLETELY** and **UTTERLY** *terrified* of watermelons!

- THE END -

How to draw Devil-Cat

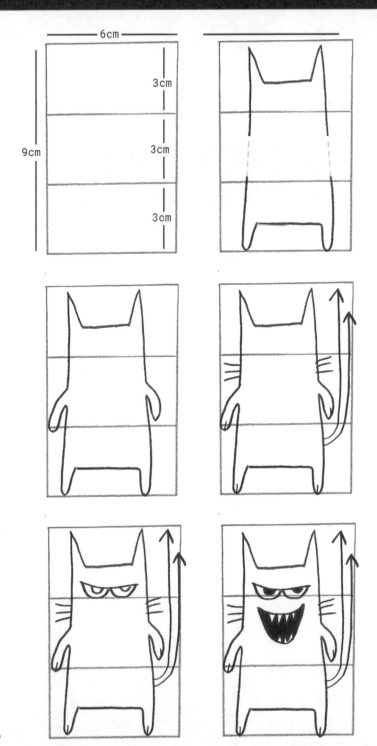

How to draw Bunny-Face

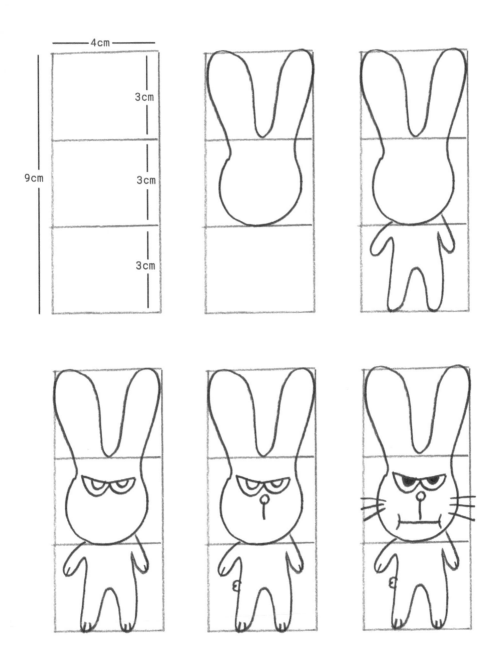

Do you want to know why Devil-Cat is *so scared of watermelons?*

The answer actually involves an exploding watermelon, but it's such a long story that it takes over 80 pages to explain!

You can read all about it in THE ADVENTURES OF DEVIL-CAT Volume 1, out now!

Smiley-Cola is the most popular cola on the market. But when Devil-Cat and Bunny-Face start selling their OWN concoctions, strange things start happening all over town.

Follow Devil-Cat's belly-busting adventures as he battles Bunny-Face for control of the milkshake market, and for glory in the World Carrot Growing Championship.

**Have you checked out our
TOTAL MAYHEM illustrated chapter book series?**

*Total Mayhem is a hilarious, action-packed,
highly-original series starring **Dash Candoo** and his
friends, as they battle the forces of evil.*

And Devil-Cat guest-stars in them too!

**Each book is a day of the week
and they are SERIOUSLY FUN!**

*"A high-octane caper"
— Publishers Weekly*

*"Delightfully chaotic"
— Kirkus Reviews*

*"Absolutely awful!"
— Mrs. Belch-Hick*

When ALL the world-famous Fluff-tailed Hemple-fluffer ducks
disappear from Zoo Lake, Dash and Rob jump into action.
They soon realise the ducks haven't just gone off on their own.
Instead, a MAJOR criminal operation (and duck-napping)
has taken place. They need to stop it, and fast!

Something is amiss at the Botanical Gardens.
Does it have anything to do with the mysterious helicopter
landings on Norma Island? That place is STRICTLY OUT OF
BOUNDS, which is why Dash and friends need to get there
fast to investigate.

The hatch was open and penguins were POURING out. "STAY CALM!"
yelled the principal, Mrs. Rosebank. "GO BACK TO YOUR
CLASSROOMS!" Dash and friends do as they're told, but when
something happens to their new classmate Ellen Ellenbogen -
linked to the world famous Ellenbogen Snausage Factory -
it's time to act, and sneriously fast.

One of the most exciting events of the year is taking place at Swedhump Elementary: Marble Day. When the grand prize gets stolen and then recovered, it seems as if all is well. But then things begin to rapidly unravel. Dash, Greta, Rob and Ellen have another mystery to solve!

It's Kite Festival Swedhump Elementary, a fantastic annual event with lots of prizes to be won. But just a few hours before the opening, a terrible discovery is made. Dash and friends need to get into action and solve the mystery, FAST, before the festival is cancelled!

The world's FUNNIEST and also MOST USEFUL joke book EVER.

743 laugh-out-loud jokes and then a HUGE INDEX at the back so you can find a joke for any occasion.

A MUST for any Total Mayhem fans, this Almanac is an INDISPENSABLE accompaniment to the books, adding TONS of new info to Dash Candoo's fantastic world.

Alphabetically-ordered for easy reference.

Did you know that we *self-published* these books ourselves?

Which is why they are only available on Amazon.

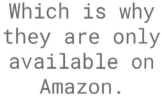

And so we want to ask you a *teeny* favor.

Actually a *teeny*, *teeny*, *TEENY*, *teeny*, *teeny*, *teeny*, *teeny*, *TEENY* one.

Made in United States
Troutdale, OR
01/09/2025

27792323R00127